Scattered Light

A Jessie Rehder Memorial Book

Scattered Light

by Christopher Brookhouse

The University of North Carolina Press
Chapel Hill
1969

Copyright ©1965, 1966, 1967, 1968, 1969 by Christopher Brookhouse
All rights reserved
Some of the poems in this volume have previously appeared in
*Advocate, ARX, Atlantic Monthly, Carolina Quarterly,
Cimarron Review, Harper's Magazine, Lillabulero, London Magazine,
Laurel Review, Latitudes, North Carolina Anvil, Shenandoah,
Southern Poetry Review,* and *Southern Review.*
Library of Congress Catalog Card Number 79-80922
Manufactured in the United States of America

for Stephen and Nathaniel

Contents

Part 1

Post Cards from California	3
New Year, 1967	5
The Children	6
Home Coming	7
Epitaph for a Child	8
Driving Through Arizona	9
Prayer	10
Woman Waking	11
Old Woman, you are like . . .	12
A 'found/unfound' definition of love	13
Eve	14
A Gesture	15
The Wolves	16

Part 2

Whitby	17
The Midway	19
Poem to the Hunters	20
Hilda and the Snakes	21
Daughters of the New England Captains	22
The Witch	23
The Finding	25

Dragons	27
Mr. Chunk	28
Five Year Old Walking	29
The Old Men	30
Buried Treasure	31
The Man in the Ocelot Suit	32

Part 3

Wintering	33
Words for shapes left outside	34
6 a.m.	35
Geometries	36
The Awakening	37
First Spring, Last Spring	38
Pastoral	39
Discourse	40
Jackson Pollock	41
Baudelaire, je pense à toi	42

Part 4

Rain	43
Easter	44

Scattered Light

Part 1

Post Cards from California

I
In Palo Alto
A field of eucalyptus
Stretched to the edge
Of the Coast Range.
I watched the afternoon
Consume the trees
And then the field,
But the shadows
Could not
Consume my eyes.

II
In Monterey
The first
Woman I ever
Loved lived in a shack
Union Pacific yellow
With thin windows
Pointed at the top.
When I went outside
With the scent of her thighs
Spilled on my hands
I was very young
But I heard the sea
Heaving and flowing
Like an old
Satisfied
Lover.

III
In Bakersfield
I met a man
Whose father
Raised raisins.
He dreamed
The raisins
Were wine.
So the old man
Came home drunk
Everyday,
Regular
You might say,
On raisin wine.

IV
In the San Diego
Zoo
The keepers
Kept
An eagle
Who ate
Himself.
The people
Gaped at the cage;
They felt vaguely
Something was wrong.

New Year, 1967

Now we hear
Clocks ticking
Heavily through
Each night, and we

Stumble between
Protests and headlines,
American soldiers
Unexpectedly brave,

Unexpectedly dead.
Behind our mind
Orphans crawl
From gutted shelters.
All ideas

Reduce to faces,
And faces to bodies;
All days to a quiet,
Complete madness.

Stiff-kneed we bend
But forget old words
Because all faces
Are real, are dead.

At last the prayer,
Not for the world;
Only for morning
And routine distractions.

The Children

The yellow lights flick on
But the children lose
Their shadows where they run

Until the moon's rising
Draws them skyward
Beyond the sprawl

Of tenements, into
A distance of stars
Where peace floats

Disembodied, outside
Terror and fragments
Until the children returning

Hear the cry of their fathers
Where the rats hunch
On the dry stairs.

Home Coming

Is this my house?
Do I only dream
The matches are gone,
The knives are hidden,
The bonded whiskies
Have been consumed.

Our daily guests
Comfort my wife.
I serve them tea.
Their smiles are faint
As a razor's edge.
That is gone too.

Our roses are late,
The market is down.
I used to talk
Of plastic graves,
Or corpses in the rain.
I thought I was sane.

I used to live
In many rooms,
Now I'm confined
To one; but I
Remember pictures
I used to have.

One showed a dove
Flying in a blue
Sky. It rained,
And doves after all
Are pigeons. Then
They took me away.

Epitaph for a Child

Someone has stolen the treasure,
Travelled the bright road,
But left no mark
If he touched
The snow,
Nor shadow
If he passed
Under the moon.
Only the cry of the hawk
Is the answer I understand.

Driving Through Arizona

I
There was no cause to stop; the road ran straight
Glutting the piston lust of slick machine;
Mesa and mountain, gaunt and seriate,
Melted in sky. My nerves sensed death, unseen,

Coiled in the sun. My hands gripped the wheel;
Slivered tongues of reptiles flicked at the mind.
Heat chafed my legs and arms; my eyes were sealed
In the hot enormity of space, and blind.

II
Late in the day I saw two Indians
Walking along the road, two figures dark
As earth. I stopped to watch, they turned, and then
Slanted across the plain toward the purple arc

Fading the mountain's rim. Father and son
Tracking the sand brittle with tribal bone,
Sand that had blunted the arrow, choked the gun—
Proud, aloof, they sought their scattered home.

I waited on the road; the sun went down.
The desert cooled, cracked in the freezing air.
The wind in the mountains beat a sullen sound;
Behind the rocks eyes shot me with their stare.

Prayer

    for K.B.

These nights I study how
This tree projects its branches
Against
My window; the leaves move toward my breath.

No sleep in this narrow bed.
The moonlight gathers the tree
Closer.
Claws cluster and beckon toward me from my wall.

These nights I remember the screaming
Dive of a plane I took once,
The thunder
Of air, the jolting slant toward death.

I had prayed, God do not let
Me die bursting and broken
With strangers.
The plane pulled up, shuddered to life.

These nights I pray for the season
To turn, for leaves falling
Off.
For unknown faces staring at me

Between branches picked clean.
I pray for the winter light
Gathering
Us all together into its darkness.

Woman Waking

Now if we shift our weight
And disentangle, the morning
Air will dry our wetness.
The sun will be wrong.

The things of your room must mark
Everywhere your separateness:
Your books or clothes,
Or shells from a coast

We will never visit together,
Or the insulting order
Of another woman's hand.
To explain is too much.

But in the darkness of my eyes
I burn to know.
At least remind me what
Names we have used.

Old Woman, you are like . . .

The mongrel outside
The flaking barroom.

Bone and sad eyes
Who might have been
The sleek watcher

Where the wolf crouched
And the flock slept
In the bright fields.

Limping hound, following
The stray through the gutters,
Luck was against you.

A 'found/unfound' definition of love

1. A feeling of
   Strong personal attachment
   Influenced by
   Sympathetic understanding
   Or
   By ties of kinship.

2. Tender and passionate
   Affection for one
   Of the opposite sex.

3. Frequently,
   Intercourse
   Itself
   With members
   Of the same,
   Or the opposite,
   Sex.

4. Nothing;
   No points scored.

Eve

I have never seen him,
Yet I know he calls
Her from his sleep,
I know his hand
Fondles the sheet

Her body has left.
She moves toward the night
Through rooms where his presence
Lingers faintly
In the fragrance of whiskey.

Then her shadow turns
Full of the force
Of her thighs to a solitary
Dance in which
No centuries intervene.

Dreaming of her nakedness,
Her husband trembles.
His sweat is cold
As a serpent pressed
Against his body.

His terror shocks
The silence; the dancer
Does not stop, and the echo
Returning is the terror
Of my own knowing.

A Gesture

She aches a little,
And the sleep he denied
Her forces its weight
Against her body.

The long rhythms
He cautiously planned
While they drank champagne,
And he made the afternoon
A slow landscape,

Sobered when she dressed.
Now she feels
His silence and the thrust
Of his Porsche around her
Taking her home.

The top is down,
So she watches the sun
Sliding deeper
Into the groves of pines.

There is nothing else
To do but press
Close to the dampness
Of her own pleasure,

Or taste the sweet
Rim of the empty
Crystal she stole
Away, and loft
The glass at the pines,

And miles down the road
Imagine the glass
Was broken, and the last
Brightness of the sun
Sparkles in the pieces.

The Wolves

Last winter, just to the north of us, the snow
Gathered to depths of fifty feet.
In layers the predator and hunted each
Congealed, wolves prowled for bones to eat.

A few slunk south limping on swollen paws;
They smelled the breath of our town and swerved.
They crouched in the street and moaned through quivering jaws.
Our children cried for their amber eyes

And clutched our pointing guns. The boys left scraps
For the lurking wolves, who ate and stayed.
On glacier nights they howled in primeval grief,
Our children pitied, unafraid.

Spring came, the wolves flowed out of town. They pranced
And choired like demons through the hills.
But now our children wake at night; entranced
By the moon they sway on hands and knees.

Part 2

Whitby

      for David Kalstone

The noon is low, the sun
Blurred like the eyes of the buried
Sailors who stumble to the sea.
A donkey paws the seaweed
Strung on the jagged beach.
The red-kneed children, wool
Thighed, stand at the North
Sea's rim. The isolation
Nulls their sense; no land
Rises beyond this shore.

Along the quay the peeling
Trawlers bob and scrape.
A prostitute gets up; her sheets
Smell like old fish. She counts
Her cash and goes outside
To watch the men mending
Their nets. She hears the buoys
Tolling; she knows fishermen
Don't talk in their sleep, but
Sometimes their eyes don't close.

The bingo parlor sagging
At the water's edge blares
Rock and numbers. Out front
The local boys, shaven and
Perfumed, sporting shoes
Dagger pointed, gesture

Sad wives to try their luck.
The gestures are routine;
The women don't resist.
They enter; they listen for the wind.

Above the quay a tourist
Sits by the ruined abbey.
He's tired of walking, tired
Of quaint decay; weary
Of the sullen, beating sea.
And he fails to care why—
The trawlers chugging out—
The little children seek
Their mothers, the slattern forgets
Her cash, the bingo stops;
The old sailors quake with new life.
Nor does he hear in the wordless
Wakes that rush on the shore,
Voices intoning farewells.

Whitby is a fishing town on the coast of Yorkshire. No one famous was born there, although Captain Cook once lived there for some years. The abbey, in ruins, attracts a few visitors. In this abbey the famous synod was held in the seventh century.

The Midway

We have a refuge here,
The price is cheap.
We are free to enter
This giddy force;
To ride the tubes
Spiraling in air,
Or the neon cage
Whirling and lashing
The sunset. Our screams
Will keep us from seeing
The sun falling
Out of the sky.

Poem to the Hunters

There must be a twilight
In the distant forests
Where old hunters walk
And their hounds follow.

A season and mind
Of solemn joy
When old hunters know
The hunting is done.

A time for dying,
When these hunters gather
Sticks and wait
With their hounds by a fire.

Hilda and the Snakes

She followed them
Through fields, where
She could not see
Them parting the grass
And vines at the root.

Her flesh quivered,
Their secret bellies
Moved. She followed
Where there was never
Path nor lane.

They never came
To her, and if
She actually caught
One in the open
It whipped to strike.

We let her wander
The fields; we never
Hindered and only
Brought her back home
On rainy September

Nights, when she stood
Shivering by the orchard
And said, "the snakes
Huddle for warmth,
They glisten and entwine."

Daughters of the New England Captains

We do not weep
In our vaulted rooms,
We live in the skins
Our fathers left us.

Each morning we put on
Their ubiquitous calm,
Which served them well
While their ships rotted out.

Our pain shall not break
Days or hearts,
Each hour confirms
The poise of silence.

At twilight descended
From the widow's walk
We meet the resolve
Of dusty eyes.

And when we pass
Through the silver evening
Of their bitter decanters,
We swallow our tears down.

The Witch

The wind off the Gulf
Convulses the palms,
Shatters the gardens.

In bed the lady
Dreams, a coffin
Floats down the air

Straight to her eyes,
Which penetrate
The lid nailed shut.

She wakes; the name
Slips like an ash
From her lips. She packs

For another funeral.
Frail and ordinary
She rides the bus.

The family gathers;
They know her dreams.
None greets her, all

Refuse her claim
As blood and kin,
Her right to mourn.

She prays for this dead,
And she would pray
To die herself,

But for her dream
Of her blood transferred,
Throbbing in the stringy

Veins of the ragged
Owl who perches
On barn or house

Foretelling death
Upon death, clutched
By an unremitting force.

The Finding

    for Kimball King

One winter at the University of Wisconsin some women from a mental hospital were taken for a swim in the university pool. One of these women left the gymnasium and froze to death outside on the lake.

I
The doors were unlocked,
And so she left.
Then she was walking
Outside in the winter
Air which was empty
And blue. She hears
No voice she knows.
The giggling bodies
Are silent in the pool.

The boy is startled
By the naked woman,
And he shrugs deeper
Into his parka
And wonders what madness
Must send her out.

She passes the yellow
Bus that has brought
The swimmers. The sun
Is too thin to melt
The wedges of ice
In the corners of the windows.

She begins to feel
A burning in the tips
Of her breasts and inside
Her thighs. She rubs
Herself there and her fingers
Seem slowly to move,

As if they belong
To someone else,
Someone not there.

II
A face is watching.
A face so like
Her own, staring up.
And when she bends
Her face closer,
The other face
Changes and smiles.
The glass reflecting
Their smiles, the surface
Wide where the wind
Has blown away
The snow, and the blue
Inverted sky
Are drawing her down,
To kiss that face.

Her lips are chilled,
And she cannot speak
To this strange love.
But she senses something
Past coming near.
An earlier self
Forgotten, untouched,
Is waiting there
In the blue of an eye
And the smiling lips
Of another life.

Her swollen hands
Spread out and she falls
In the arms of a child
Who has died in the ice.

Dragons

What did dragons dream?

>   that rattly men
>   sheathed and riveted
>   forsook all vows
>   and stayed at home?
>
>   that all creatures drank
>   their fill from mirrors
>   beside scented roads?
>   that kind thought grass
>   sweeter than flesh?
>
>   that spears rusted;
>   that tongues of flame
>   cooled to clouds, vanished?
>
>   Ah, my dragons,
>   Why did you wake?

Mr. Chunk

Tonight I cannot sleep.
A voice returns in the holly
Trees and a bright presence
Whispers in the frosty pines.

My bear and fox are not
Asleep. He has come back.
The bear holds our journey
In his solitary eye.

We waited for him all summer
While he slept in the deep forest
And awoke slowly in changing
Skies and the falling leaves.

Now we will slip quietly
Down empty halls among
The darkness where others sleep.
Our journey is always cold.

The bear peers forward, the fox
Keeps watch over my shoulder.
Then we are there. His greeting
Bursts up and his red flame dances

And our shadows dance behind us.
He puffs and glows in my cheeks.
I embrace my bear and fox,
Closing our shadows into one.

Five Year Old Walking

We are ready to go,
He straps the gun
Against his side.

Charms must replace
Each other, today
A green revolver

Clicking at shadows
Which move in the meaning
He gives to them.

He is shaggy and quick,
And on this day
His aim is deadly.

He wants to know
What do I bring
To shoot at the shadows,

And if at noon
I see darkness
In the bright fields.

The Old Men

It is the sign
Of age; the vision
Fails. The print

Of banana empires
Falling and distant
Clashes at borders,

Or the catastrophe
Of scattered war
Diminishes, the pages

Go blank. But the old men
Need not read
Their histories,

They sense disaster
On every continent.
They are tired of knowing.

They walk by themselves
And watch the birds
Flicker in the sun.

And when the birds
Are only shadows,
And the men are blind

At last, they touch
The earth and lie
In its dark furrows.

Buried Treasure

In nineteen twenty-seven, in New York,
A girl of nine frilled in her blue lace robe
Passes her parents' door; the Sunday sun
Rouges the watchful shepherds on the wall.

Under the canopy weightlessly arching
The winding spirals of mahogany,
Her father's hand rests by her mother's cheek;
Her mother's fragrance softens the rosy air.

The child descends the stair, careful to skip
Over the squeaks hushed by the saffron runner.
The servants are not up; the only sound
Is from her robe rustling from room to room.

She stands before a fireplace; the dogs
Lap at her hem with iron tongues. She dares
To taste the champagne caught in a crystal glass.
Then she bends down, draws back the edge of leaves

Woven to vines, and lifts a stone from the hearth.
Out of her pocket she slips a milk-blue marble,
Strokes it upon her sleeve until the roundness
Glows like a gem, shines like a sleeping face.

She gives her treasure to this hearth, and tugs
The stone into place.

The Man in the Ocelot Suit

Our neighbor's dog ate
Our paper. My wife
Complained. They said get up
Earlier, go to work.

What do you do all night?
My wife said
We think grave thoughts, and laugh
Against establishments.

The dog kept eating the paper,
So I rented
An ocelot suit and sprang
Out of a ditch. The terrified

Dog never came back,
But our neighbors
Came, breathing hard, and ate
The paper themselves to set

Us straight and make the world
Safe from crackpots.
Now I loaf in my sleek
Ocelot suit, amusing the children.

When it is night,
I leap onto our neighbor's
Roof and devour their dreams.

Part 3

Wintering

There are eyes among the sedge,
And eyes along the branches,
And eyes that peer above
The slate flatness of the pond,
And all these eyes watch
The drift of scattered light.

A few late birds beat south.
They are lost in the sky like smoke
Blown from my stone chimney.
The hills are vast and silent.
Snow will fall soon; the deer
Will nudge my door to lick

Salt from my hand; and beasts
Will turn from their solitary hunts
And sleep in the warm shadows
Of their enemies. And I
Will sit at the edge of fire.
I will be safe from cold.

But my knife shines in my hand:
How easy to slice this flesh
And watch it open and spread.
I will hear the long breathing
From the deep dens of animals.
I winter in my own shadow.

Words for shapes left outside

Autumn and you go away
And leave us here
In your garden. Weeds
Thicken on our stakes.

Where crows return
No more, mice
Scuttle down fallen
Rows, and a hawk

Watches from the yellow
Sky. Then winter
Freezes in our throats,
And we hang from nails

In the hats and coats
Of your own outgrowing.
We are always thus
Something of yourselves.

Don't you ever see
When the snow breaks
The weeds and buries
The bones of the mice

Our rags blown
Like shadows on the wind,
Or how snow deepens
Behind you in your tracks.

6 a.m.

Past my window
A crow is flying,
His dipping wings
Crisp in the light.

The end of his flight
Is a hill beyond
My view, his essence
Is his flying.

But you, my child,
Who drops sighing
Asleep in my arms,
You will be told

Your essence is more
Than motion, is not
The flying in the cold
Days of this light.

One morning you will wake
With the full weight
Of cold upon you,
Then all is the flight.

Geometries

We love
Because of the shadow
Of the hawk's wing
When he hunts on the mountain.

Because our flesh stings
In all the blind oceans
Pulling us down.

Because each afternoon
Dies in dark triangles,
So like our own.

The Awakening
>for Max Steele

Dear Max,
In your arms your son
Dreams in his nest of sleep.

His cry has gone
Past the white morning,
Pines, and falling stars.

But walking in this room
You hear him past hearing,
In all the familiar

His cry choking
In his soft throat.
Nothing is the same.

The silences fail,
A branch breaks,
The hunter steps forth
And shrugs in the cold.

First Spring, Last Spring

Turning out the door,
A face
I have not seen before.

In pools of melting snow,
A sign
I am afraid to know.

In glistening avenues
A truth;
The beauties we pursue

At last are the long skies
Moving
Where we have frosted eyes.

I know it was my face,
Lost
In this cold and sudden grace.

Pastoral

I have lost count of time.
My life is only the sun,
Or the thin rising of the moon.

I fly with the heron and travel
These hills where the trees sparkle
After the rain. I sleep in the silence
Of rocks and the darkness of the den.

But on that morning I do not wake,
A gleaming hawk will circle
Down to taste my eyes.

Discourse

Let me work on this logic,
What is beautiful
Is inevitable in the time
Space or sky
Where it exists,
And no where else—

Like driftwood breaking
The long emptiness
Of a beach. It would not
Be the same if rocks
Intruded, then chance
Left the driftwood there.

Can this be turned around?
What is inevitable
Is beautiful. No,
Then you would believe
In unreasonable destructions
As well as love.

Jackson Pollock
    in a photograph by Hans Namuth

The patches of grass around him
Are dry, as if all summer
No rain has eased the earth.
Beyond the pasture in which
He sits the trees become
The shadows. There is no wind.
There are no clouds in the sky.

He is looking at the grass
And not looking. He has
Come out of his studio and not
Come out. His eyes contract
With pain. His body is flexed
Like a fighter, but he slumps down
To the dying grass. The cigarette
Burns at the tip of his fingers.

The watcher knows more than this.
There is a chance of rain
Which the moment does not suggest,
A wetness to soften the landscape,
A wind to move the trees.
Nature is unheroic.
Each leaf and spike of grass
Will reproduce its own self,
Or simply die without pain.

Baudelaire, je pense à toi

The beggars still shake
Sleep from their eyes,
And the black Seine
Washes their feet.

Novelists still write what sells,
Painters decorate the rich;
The hands of wasted poets
Tremble and their words spill.

But on a summer morning
Your ghost escapes
This pain, and where you go
Through avenues and across bridges
It is the Paris of the children,
Where the carrousel turns and its music
Rises into the trees.

Part 4

Rain

I knew
Eventually the rain
Would rot this house,
And the weight
Of the sky would fall
Among the mountains,
The birds leave
No songs
In the gray trees.

I knew
Eventually the rain
Would dissolve each
Patch of cloth, and flesh
Slip from its bones.
I knew my eyes would lie
Blue and diluted,
Fixed on the clouds.

Easter

I
I wake before dawn
In the watch of the crow
And lie listening

Inside the last darkness
To the wind in the hills.
But there is something

Prowling the darkness,
And I know it crouches
Beside me with the sun
In its yellow eyes.

II
The southern morning spreads
Through the green webs of April.
The finches rise in golden
Circles and sing from the trees

While I am singing in my skin.
My blood beats as if without
End, and my fingers touch
My solitary flesh burning

And exquisite. I was flesh,
I am, and I shall be.
I press my blood into
The open greed of time.

III
My neighbors returning
From services wave
Their potted lilies.

I am deep in the earth
Planting blood-red
Perennials. My children

Are away playing in the hills.
I am alone
To labor here.

And if I sense the insistent
Presence of something
Who smells my soul,

I will not turn and see.
If it is Christ the tiger,
He has come before.

I will place my gifts to this earth
Within the earth, and I know
This earth is my only home.

www.ingramcontent.com/pod-product-compliance
Lightning Source LLC
Chambersburg PA
CBHW031715230426
43668CB00006B/223